BETWEEN THE CHAINS

Phoenix Poets

A SERIES EDITED BY ROBERT VON HALLBERG

TURNER CASSITY

BETWEEN THE CHAINS

THE UNIVERSITY OF CHICAGO PRESS

Chicago and London

Turner Cassity was born in 1929 in Jackson, Mississippi. He is the author of seven books of poetry, including Hurricane Lamp (also published in the Phoenix Poets series).

The University of Chicago Press, Chicago 60637
The University of Chicago Press, Ltd., London
© 1991 by The University of Chicago
All rights reserved. Published 1991
Printed in the United States of America

00 99 98 97 96 95 94 93 92 91   5 4 3 2 1

Library of Congress Cataloging-in-Publication Data

Cassity, Turner.
    Between the chains / Turner Cassity.
        p.   cm. — (Phoenix poets)
    ISBN 0-226-09616-5 (cloth). — ISBN 0-226-09617-3 (pbk.)
    I. Title.   II. Series.
    PS3558.A8B4   1991
    811'.54—dc20   90-49168
                                                          CIP

⊗ The paper used in this publication meets the minimum requirements of the American National Standard for Information Sciences—Permanence of Paper for Printed Library Materials, ANSI Z39.48-1984.

Paperback cover illustration: Paul Outerbridge, Ide Collar, The Metropolitan Museum of Art, Ford Motor Company Collection, Gift of the Ford Motor Company and John C. Waddell, 1987 (1987.1100.462). Courtesy of G. Ray Hawkins Gallery.

In memory of
Mary Davenport Spiva
1906–1985

"We are too used to the idea of work to realise its meaning," said Hugo. "I had early suspicions of it, and dared to act on them."

"What a comment on life," said Lavinia, "that to be out of work is held to be sad and wrong!"

"Satan lies in wait for idle hands," said Selina.

"But only Satan, Grandma. And he is hardly seen as a model of behaviour."

I. Compton-Burnett
The Mighty and Their Fall

Contents

Acknowledgments

Grateful acknowledgment is made to the following publications in which many of these poems first appeared.

Chicago Review: "Lazy Afternoon."
Cumberland Review: "Links."
Drastic Measures: "Acid Rain on Sherwood Forest," "Some People Have No Small Talk," "Franchises," "An Attempt to Explain Anorexia Nervosa to Lillian Russell."
Fontana: "Power Failure," "Publicans and Sinners."
Formalist: "Sketch for an Edda."
Local Storms: Section IV of "Atlantis of the Conchs" under the title "Deep Depression in Key West."
Lullwater Review: "Quasimodo of the Singing Tower," "Betsy Ross, Astronaut," "Texarkana."
Poetry: "Persistence of Memory," "Prometheus in Polynesia," "Inducted," "Other Directed."
Sequoia: "Open Wounds," "Between the Chains."
Sewanee Review: "Hedy Lamarr and a Chocolate Bar," "Berlin-to-Baghdad."
Yale Review: "How Jazz Came up the Elbe," "Preservation News," "For the Scrapbook of Mrs. Charles Black."
Keys to Mayerling (chapbook; published by R. L. Barth): "Atlantis of the Conchs."

Lessons (by R. L. Barth and Turner Cassity; published by Para Press): "Bank Notes."

Mainstreaming: Poems of Military Life (by R. L. Barth, Turner Cassity, and Warren Hope): "Mainstreaming," "Campion in Uniform."

The Music of His History: Poems for Charles Gullans on His Sixtieth Birthday (edited by Timothy Steele; published by R. L. Barth): "When in Doubt Remain in Doubt."

Persistence of Memory

What is it that a string around the finger says?
  Remember? No.
Remember to remember. It is Fool's Regress:

Our little act of distancing that, ruse enough,
  Will bring up front
Such dark and backward as we otherwise repress,

Once tedium begins to do the work of time.
  Trash, payments, locks,
Abysses all; and, worse, birthdays in middle age.

No fool forgets to order lobster, chill champagne.
  Might that occur
His aide-mémoire had better be a cordon rouge.

For double duty, heavy duty, handcuffs serve—
  After the fact.
The chains of masochism prompt. Is it the mind?

And if they come, hospital or the gallows, like
    Detail to crowd
Then wholly to estrange the one detail our life,

Mnemonics at the end will bring it flooding back.
    Around the arm
The bracelet with the dose; around the neck the noose.

Hedy Lamarr and
a Chocolate Bar

Showings are six a day, continuous.
No need to wait in line or be on time;
In any case the plot will be generic:
Boy meets. Scorning the concession stand
(I am austere, for not much more than twelve),
Unfed by choice I go to meet the dark.
Algiers a frame or two before the end,
And in her big close-up Gaby departs,
Rogue Helen at the railing of a ship,
To wreck the blood as on the wall of Troy.
It is a vision that transfixes. Gel,
Dead center in the aisle, I cannot move
So long as ecstasy stares out ahead.
The vision vanishes, and Charles Boyer
Comes on to suffer who cares what. By now
I am so shaken that I turn around,
Retrace my steps, and thank the taste of Mars.
If, showings later, I become aware
That my experience is every man's,
And every man, if *she* is on the screen,
Is rooted in the aisle as I was, too
Exanimate to stumble toward a seat,

It does not mean that under Mitterrand
I womanize. And at our age who wants
Algeria. But I know what I know.
I have seen beauty stop men in their tracks.

Prometheus in Polynesia

The beachboys douse the flambeaux; at the tideline it is dark.
Log drums—contemporary, but no matter—thunder out
Abstractions of the storm and heartbeat, surf outside the reef,
Heights' very sound of seismic fire. As if the drum were god,
Force creates of itself a flesh full grown: a wisdom male,
Not of the forehead but the fingertips. His two batons
Ablaze at either end, a dancer leaps in light he mocks.
You could not possibly explain to him what hubris is.
If fire is of the air, not theft but gift; is of the rock
Inside the crater as it reddens, he who masters it
Is not a prisoner, not priest. He is a twirler. Change
His sex and there is something of a tassel dancer there.
Drum major in a lava-lava, puppeteer whose strings,
Whose puppets are the fire, he is not quite invisible,
Nor would he wish to be: footlights he juggles in his hands.
Whose is revenge? If any vengeance gnaws his liver out
It's that of rum. Not, though, just yet. A torso's fabled ease
Reminds us that the will and vision of the primitive
Can be taught nothing by the stroboscope. The torch outspeeds
Its own blaze. Orbit of our vanity, the fire goes free.
In figure eights the orange salamander bites its tail.

Full circles smooth and feather. In their going, coming flame
The dancer freezes in his postures speed makes visible.
Greek fool, fool of the Renaissance who huddle by the lamp,
If lava grips who uses it, it is no eagle's claw.
It is an Oversoul in pleasure taking back its own.

When in Doubt,
Remain in Doubt

Not even on the eve of Salamis
Did Delphi give a competent response.
No oracle does, ever. That is why
Great Men consult them. Oracles are doubt
Objectified, but left ambiguous,
So as to force a choice. In scrap-iron pomp
And strength of China's gold, the Emperor,
In mid-November 1941,
Has entrails made of plastic summoned, quick
To tell him "Let the punishment befit
The crime." And so the secret task force sails.
Commanders Short and Kimmel, one might add,
Did not consult, not even one another.
May of 1945. As Saul
Sought out the Witch of Endor, in a smoke
Filled room in Kansas City Harry Truman
Hears exotic dancers speak in tongues.
The meaning is not clear, but just may be
"Waste not, want not," of which one must assume
H. heard the first fourth only, as he wastes
Hiroshima and Nagasaki. Some,
Including me, do not do oracles,

But we aren't great. And of the cities two
It's Nagasaki I should like to see,
For reasons having not to do with bombs
But with Puccini. *Trust in wooden walls.*
It's they which have the best acoustics, Del;
And if the Persians come (Iranians),
Or have the bomb, is stone more sheltering?

Acid Rain on Sherwood Forest

The longbow, one would say, is natural;
Is an appropriate technology.
The crossbow is the downward path to Krupp.
It has a trigger, eyepiece; has a stock
Firearms have learned from. One would say. One would,
However, be quite wrong, as Baron Krupp
Might point out. Compound bows are anything
But natural, as they are laminate,
And what is natural about a graft?
We have, as usual, let sentiment
Define the natural. Our sympathies
Are not with progress but with Robin Hood,
Who is himself mere envy wearing tights.
What has redistribution of the wealth
To do with archery? It was the Krupps
Who had the world's first pension plan, and built
Its first real worker housing. Had *sick leave?*
We cannot speculate what was the life
Of Merry Men grown old. The arrow flies,
An infantry's or Time's, and how the wound
Arrives is of no consequence. Had Cain
No weapons but his hands he would be Cain,

And Abel dead of strangulation. Child
Of nature, little boy of five or six,
Why have you pulled the rubber suction cup
From off your arrow and begun to sharpen it?

Bank Notes

Parnassian in its simplicity of greed,
The Banque de l'Indo-Chine, obdured in privilege,
A presence on the distant side of two world wars
And two republics, looks increasingly to be,
Of their and our more recent wars, a clear first cause.
If Indochina in the 30s is a lost
Atlantis, it is Aristotle's, not Plato's,
In that the vision and the ruin most submerged
Is its Prime Mover. Out of undertows profound
But all too scrutable—come at the beckoning
Of justice and of so much blood—the Bank appears.
It is in mint condition, having been the Mint,
Or Bureau of Engraving at the very least.
Its currency, as the Depression deepens, holds
Its value, having never been exchangeable
For that of France, and keeping to a specie rate
When France devalues. As immediate result,
Hanoi and Saigon have the most expensive shops
In Europe or in Asia, and the fewest sales,
As rubber and as sugar will not sell abroad,
And planters have no money. Cruise ships give wide berth;
Angkor gives in to bats it is the color of.
No crash concerns the Bank, whose chief activities

Are lobbying in Paris, kept up on a scale
That would embarrass de Lesseps in Panama,
And speculating in Shanghai. The Privilege,
Renewed for "five-and-twenty years" in '22,
Protects it absolutely from the Bank of France,
No model of responsibility itself,
But not an international mah-jong concern.
Vichy both understand at once. The Japanese
Do not disturb them, knowing that it was the banks
Who pressured Vichy to admit them. As they stage
For Luzon and for Singapore, the Bank calls due
Its notes on Royal Dutch and the Batavia
Exchange, another background noise imperiling
Pearl Harbor. Policy and war much isolate
A colony that serves two masters warily,
But not to the extent the high exchange rate did.
Behind that silver barrier, at their own speed,
Away from Western eyes, a thousand opiates
Grow strong; and poppies, red however, are not red
Without companionship. The sugar in the fields
Rots into rum; the rubber dies above the graft.
The private Bank has never skipped a dividend.
On schedule, monsoon rains sweep warm and colorless
Across the Saigon River into New Saigon.
Inane canaries droop on concrete balconies.
Hats, hollow in the crown, deluge and cool the hair,
Protect the eyes in wide straw circles from the wet.
Tricycle wheels make grayish egrets in the street.
It rains in gray side streets as never in the heart.
A continent . . . subcontinent? . . . side continent
Once more is going under. There is this to say
Of it and of its Bank whose creature from the first
It was: it moved its funds from where its mouth had been.
So many decades later, did the U.S.A.?

Correction and
Amplification

> Boudin, *the dark, unbelievably hot sausage beloved of the Legionnaires, is unknown outside North Africa.*
>
> Charles E. Mercer, *Legion of Strangers*

High stumps that were the palm trees are the lights;
The low palmettos fence the stadium.
The high-school football team of Lafayette,
Louisiana, runs out on the field
In contact lenses and an endless text
Of Cajun names. It is the Catholic
High school; a jewelry of Crosses tics
Among the cheering section and the band,
Whose majorettes are Vietnamese. A priest—
Ex-chaplain, or of some sophistication—
Sees to it the pom-pom is confined
To two cheerleaders, who are blond and male.
The buzzing mildness of the winter night
Is all we have of Indochina; that,
And rattling in the unbeheaded palms.
Sahara is the stronger presence felt,
Although the locals have no sense of it.
Although the caps are not the kepi quite,
It's

    Hot Boudin! Cold Coosh-Coosh!
    Lafayette Our Savior! Push! Push! Push!

The south of I-10 vowels make the rhyme,

And couscous here is cornbread. Boudin, though,
Is boudin, even if it's made with pork,
And with the pig's unspeakables at that.
Our Savior's opposition does not flinch.
A little of the march-or-die is there,
As well it might be. That opposing team
Is Algiers High. Algiers, Louisiana,
Opposite downtown New Orleans,
But post-colonial is where you look,
And if the march sounds French, all marches do.
Take back the pom-pom, Girls; Algiers, rip up
The infidel and make that next first down.

Marquis de Lafayette knew revolution too.

How Jazz Came up the Elbe

Among composers, who best understood
Sex? Having grown up in a brothel, Brahms,
Of course. At least once he tried everything,
To have thereafter no great interest.
In any case his Schumann family,
Poor Robby-One-Note and that fertile wife,
Could have put any man off marriage.
Of his contemporaries, he alone
(You may add Wagner) missed out syphilis.
Is it that each had such a practiced eye?
The tensions in the music—Brahms', I mean—
Are neither sexual nor those of form
Through content overstressed. They are in some
Sense social: urges to tell less than all,
As witnessed by his scores which he tore up,
In opposition to his frank desire
To be Beethoven. Hannes, as care can,
Had it both ways. Along the waterfront
He had been bouncer, trick, and pianist,
As a result of which, in his old age,
Had he not thought them fools, he could have taught
Hair-raising holds to Nineties decadents.

Mad Ludwig may have put his patronage
On the wrong horse. Whorehouse and waterfront,
However, do not figure in the work,
Unless you count the *Liebeslieder Walzer.*
There he knew his *Kitsch,* price, porn, our cherub.
Carefully, he made another life.
His legend has it, though, that at the end
He would have liked to write ragtime. As pale,
Perhaps, as Broadway Weill or Berlin Jazz?
No, do not sell the uptight Master short.
If he did not know Storyville, who did?

Preservation News

High Middle Ages are the 1856
Of Eugène Viollet-le-Duc. At Notre Dame
The flying buttresses, the Victor Hugo front,
Its statuary, all are his, and well they are.
No one would look a second time at what he found.
How will the restoration-minded deal with us?
Add turret roofs, one fondly hopes, to all the Bau-
and Lever Haus and putty-up the Henry Moores.
In any case they first must have a formula,
Their working vision of what urban modern is;
If not the Virgin set against the dynamo,
Some prairie wizard in the City Emerald.
Each surface that we care for they will strip away,
And, bravely, in the space-defining voids we leave,
Lay bricks, or place-in what they have instead of urns.
Yet when they finish they will have a century
More nearly us than we have, since it can conform
More fully to the pure ideal. Art need not work.
And if they stand the Chrysler needle upside down
Upon the Empire State, if those are each rescued
From ruin, let it be. Components have a life
Their contexts may or may not share. Had we not, Kong?

What tenants when we die will know if airships did
Or did not anchor on the present TV mast?
At full stride on the road of yellow brick, lost—sure,
However, sorcery and glass will guide her home—
Can Dorothy have known that what she hurried toward
Was Berlin 1922 Expressionism?

Quasimodo of the Singing Tower

*Through the superbly beautiful architecture of the
Tower, through the music of the bells, to reach out to
the people and fill their souls with the quiet, the re-
pose, the influence of the beautiful.*

Edward W. Bok

Eliciting support from public schools,
A telethon has paid for surgery
To straighten-out the back, and grants in aid
Have been cosmetic for the face. Sweet bells
A console jangles more or less in tune;
He need not swing on ropes. Two therapists
Are making progress, although haltingly,
In dealing with the speech impediment.
An Esmeralda of a singles bar
Is an attempt at rescue now and then.
Only a shadow-spine does not respond.
The sun of Florida beats through the grills
Of faience, trapping on the bell-stage floor
Hump, back, and the incorrigible form
That are the shade of years change cannot light.
Inseverably hurt the shadow falls,
And on a day of consonants and rain,
Of exercises and the guided tour,
As quarry cornered, it will repossess.
Its spastic fist will pound the manual;
Have carillon give out a twelve-tone row.
And down the new facade, from the improved
Onto improvers, streams the molten lead.

Sketch for an Edda

The marshes of the delta fall behind;
Oars out, the Viking flagship, as the current
Dies, dies in the water. Then the oars
Thrash downward, and the dragon on the prow
Rears in a sea which is no sea. Norse strength
Has penetrated to the Caspian.
On shore the tents of local khans seduce;
The mosques of what will be Baku fix course.
And at the end, across a southern shore,
Norwegian mountains tower out of Persia.
Home in the wooded heights so full of snow
The desert-loving Persians shun them, furs
In place on pectorals the snow has burned,
A landing party climbs. By russet straw
Off cedars which are dying, tigers move:
An orange shift among the conifers;
In that contracting universe a shift
Indicative of some beginning time,
For they are Sabre Tooth. No more unknown
Than would be other tigers, to crews Norse,
But even so no trophy figurehead.
The tiger vanishes, an epic glimpse
At Persian pomp; the Vikings stay to trade.
Extinction never hurries. Dragons lived.

Ruth Keelikolani

(1883)

At something over twenty-seven stone,
The Princess Ruth, the fattest and the richest
Woman in Hawaii, in a steel
Sedan chair, is transported by a force
Of many alternating bearers, thralls
Of rupture, up the slopes of Mauna Kea,
There to sacrifice a final time
To Pele, who is fire. The Princess's
So many cousins recently have died,
Or married missionaries. She alone
Holds to the old Hawaiian ways. Taboos
Are to be broken, maybe, but not mocked.
The sacrifice is of its time and place,
A bit as if the Widow Windsor went
To search for Albert in a crater, and,
Not finding him, ignited all the tins,
Tobacco tins, on which the Prince appears.
The Princess wears a dress of black brocade
Much hung about with beads of jet. Bark cloth
And Polynesian plume is very well,
But there is simply not enough of it.
You cannot wind a world in a sarong.

Her leis she has cautiously immersed
In kerosene, and sulphur matches wait
Should Pele prove too feeble. Diving-boys
Of other days are portly diplomats
In frock coats, but a pyromaniac
Is where you find him, as the Princess Ruth
Is priestess only to a point. Her will
Is made. Her infinite and noble rents
Go to her cousin Bernice Bishop, thence
Into the Bishop Trust, "to educate
Those of Hawaiian blood."
                                 Hawaiian youth
Upon your surfboard, brown bikinied maid
Upon a low-fat diet, can you have,
Ever, that grace of continuity
Your barren, vast old benefactress had?

On Several Photographs of Nikola Tesla

Platonic forms most certainly do not exist,
And archetypes may not. What we mistake for them
Are true originals repeated down the years.
We do not chase a far ideal. We plagiarize.
And here, among his lightnings and his glass retorts,
The maddest scientist. We know him instantly,
From lurid illustrations in a thousand pulps,
And film vampires with Balkan accents. He in fact
Is Serbian, and is inventing wirelessness
And alternating current. If his name's obscure,
Marconi plagiarizes too, and Edison,
Although at one time Tesla had publicity.
He, never they, moreover, has the deeper fame
Of pure cliché, which is the figure Pop Art has
In place of archetype. True, Edison appears
Repeatedly in Norman Rockwell, but it's less
As Edison than as the Wizard Oz. No form
Predicts, no art repeats what Tesla will become:
A mild old lunatic obsessed increasingly
In feeding pigeons. He was said to have derived
Invisibility; he has become himself
Invisible. Plato, much more at ease—at home—
Among dimensions other than the ones that are,

Could not have dealt with actual invisibility.
(Make, if you like, my extra iamb disappear.)
He would, though, well have known this tall young scientist
In tie and tails, who in pursuit of some ideal,
Or future pigeons, jilted J. P. Morgan's daughter.
How mad can you be, you mad Serb scientist?
And you, Plato, how little relevant to form?
The archetypal *philosophe,* Diogenes,
Is in his barrel with a blazing DC lamp
In search of that which any fool knows not to be.
His barrel is in turn the fire of Dagon, whose
Is that one belly at which navel-gazers gaze:
The form of heartburn, as the Godhead's circling dove
Makes first an item on the menu, is a squab.

Inducted

Socialist realism paints the "Tax of Blood"
As Herod at the slaughter of the innocents,
Vast Turks impaling Christian children on their swords,
Ravishing mothers, tearing infants off the breast,
And, in the middle distance, torching granaries.
The burning grain fields are of course a scene generic,
Useful equally for World Wars I and II,
Teutonic Knights at Novgorod, the Japanese
About to starve Port Arthur. As to why these Turks
Should care to burn the possibility of tribute,
Art does not comment. Outside the gallery
Marxism of a local form has done its work
Attractively. The town is bright and circumspect,
If, by the river, obviously Ottoman.
It is provincial irreducibly, its youth,
Unlike the youth of Belgrade, innocent of jeans.
In pairs and trios they carve tree trunks and are bored.

Admit it, tractor artist; neither I nor you
Can carve a true initial in a local wood,
As much as small towns bore us. Take an alias.
Imagine you are me imagining the scene.
Our small wistaria adds blue drops to the water;
In its fragrance, gaunt, a Turkish officer,
Itinerant draft board of one, is offered çay
Upon a table-tray. Drawn up in front of him,
Four adolescents and their father. "Tell me which,"
In Bulgar says the Moslem. "I need only one."
"The eldest has good teeth," the father volunteers.
Oedipal conflicts do not have their only site
In Macedonia, the which the officer
Is quite aware, if not exactly in those terms.
That sibling staircase, notes he, has one riser missing.
Is he hidden in a cave, the favorite?
"We do not bite our foe. What of the cloven chin?"
"Left-handed, and the youngest knows the tongue of sheep.
I need him for the flocks."
                                        "And at the best of times
You farmers have one son right-handed out of three.
Choose. Let the ambidextrous pick among themselves."
He well knows who the pick will be; the cleft of chin
Has winked two times at him, and with his either eye.
"Should you consult your other brother?" says the Turk.

· · · · · · · · · ·

A last hill edging all the golden hills of Thrace,
And past it, for a gaunt recruiter and his troop,
Rise up the ruin of the Land Wall like a scarp,
And like the letters of an unknown alphabet
The minarets and domes lined on the Golden Horn.

A gypsy by the gate is dancing with some bears;
A sherbet seller, massive pitcher on his back,
Is bowing double, to defer, or start the flow.
It will be thirty years before the new recruit,
The new initiate, allows his home a thought,
And he will think then of the blue wistaria
That in the water sheds its days toward Istanbul,
And counts the days of youth, in whom the tax of blood,
So irresistible, is paid and overpaid.

Berlin-to-Baghdad

(Constantinople, 1876)

The rail construction nears Seraglio Point,
And where the beach, already narrow, ends
Below the harem seawall, German care
Decides to send a diver down. If piers
Are necessary, one must sample cores.
The diver, in his complicated suit
That, as the helmet meets it, might well seem
Mode's rubber janissary uniform,
Iron turban, dips into the Bosporus,
A non-Leander of a cautious firm.
The double current, where the Marmara
Runs on the bottom warmly north, and where
On top of it Medea's wild Black Sea
Pours south, disorients him in its chop,
But on the bottom there is blue and peace,
And there is horror. In his first surprise
He inadvertently bites off his air,
And only when his jaw relaxes frees
His intake valve to breathe. In front of him,
As if enormous tulips sprouted heads,
A score of women, sewn-up to the neck

In weighted canvas bags, and with their hair
Threading the current where it steadies, move
From side to side like Humpty-Dumpstresses.
He jerks a rope to be drawn up; he knows,
As he ascends, the garden he has seen
Is truer image of the Straits, and heart,
Than Sestos or Abydos, and that he,
And all his crewmen, and the sultanate
Of all the world have each in their own way
Numbered, bagged, and tossed. The Lorelei
So many times repeated there below,
So quietly beckoning, is small revenge.
Assistants help him screw his helmet off;
He turns it over and is sick in it.

Immurings

The land walls of Byzantium, the Maginot
Line of their time, and that time was a thousand years,
Expressways parallel today and on-ramps breach.
The highways, frankly, have the more impressive scale,
And certainly are more an obstacle, as in
Berlin the structures for the viewing of the Wall
Exceed the Wall. The Wall of China is at least
As cogent as it ever was, which is not very.
Say it is a sort of contour line gone wrong,
And may well cease beyond its last hill in the view.
The wall of walls, the self-enclosing self-enclosed—
Great serpent, seamless mouth, broad bitten tail of stone—
Is Cartagena of the Indies, whose main gate
Is tower for a clock, as if to say that time
Besieges always; is the sieging-engine, brute,
By whose monotony the first defenses crack,
And is the treachery by which a culture falls.
It is the matrix out of which technology
Is catapulted, and the cauldron out of which
The napalm and the Greek Fire pour. Not that a wall
As concept can be superseded. Cells have walls,
In brains as well as prisons. Thought and speech, at base,
Themselves are barriers, or could not be defined.

The final barrier, mere space, is absolute
And is at hand: the universe's end is hid;
The words upon this page a single space divides.
Ex-space, dry moats in Istanbul are garden plots;
The tunnels in the Maginot deep truffle runs.

Power Failure

In Parktown in Johannesburg,
Along the season-facing ridge,
The mansions of the Randlords fall to time;

Or, too granitic to destroy,
Defy the clinics, fast-foods, shops.
In this one, lordly, Thomas Cullinan,

For whom the diamond is named,
Converted carats into brick,
Or pyramided common on preferred.

In that one, co-conspirators
Are rumored to have planned, if planned
Is not too strong a word, the Jameson Raid.

In all of them, on summer days,
Wide-open windows suck the dust;
The lightning flashes as the current fails:

On dark terrazzo, cubic hail
Keeps up a dice game. At their back
And out of sight beyond the vacant mines,

In other thunder, shining tin,
The vast Southwestern Townships—East
Los Angeles strung out along the Rand—

Go bright, one streetlight to a block.
The one-eye hot plates heat the meals;
In Parktown, as the hail rounds into rain,

High candelabra light the trays,
High teapots shape the lightning flash.
The grid is not so blown it will not fuse;
The evening not so charged it will not clear.

Between the Chains

*Brokers and their clients and hangers-on would con-
gregate in the short section of Simmonds Street
between Market and Commissioner streets. The Min-
ing Commissioner had posts erected and chains hung
between them in order to close the area. Hence the
'open air Stock Exchange' and the phrase 'Between
the chains.'*

John R. Shorten, *The Johannesburg Saga*

It neither shames us nor is gain,
The broker's cry from chain to chain.

It is the human urge to trade,
Our standoff with the urge to aid.

If by it bleeding hearts are wrecked
I am not; you aren't. Nor was Brecht.

Up, Mahagonny in the claims,
And dig. Life has a digging's aims.

Here is the only city built
On neither trade nor sand nor silt

But on the rock itself of gold.
It is not, it will not be, old.

It holds much guilt, some hope, all pains,
Between the chains, between the chains.

R.U.R. or Are You Aren't?

The miners huddle in their rising cage,
A self-consolidating other. Small
Stockholders whom Anglo-American
Is eager to impress, we foreign four
Observe a changing of the shifts. It may
Be barbarous, but no one on the Rand
Supposes gold to have become a relic.
I can read my fellow goldbug's mind.
Having observed, correctly, that the streets
It drove us through are Lang's *Metropolis,*
The Company, she hopes, employs robots.
She is our mover of initiatives.
A scissor gate squeaks open; checking-off,
Lang's white mine captain gathers-in the lamps.
We shall have now the robot *Trauermarsch.*
Or shall we? At the very "point in time"
Hot shower and a whisky cross my mind,
I notice in their golddust-blasted eyes,
Beyond the utter weariness of bone,
A look I know, a lifting of the chin.
I too have drunk what is genteelly known
As Bantu beer; I know the tactile quick
That as one peels it off is boots and socks.

(How late the Board Room limo comes to call!)
Our Lady of the *République* Weimar,
I deconstruct you. Theirs a look I know,
You know. It is the sun below the yardarm,
Signaling the day may yet be saved.

Parlor Song
(1958)

"**A**nd at the border of the Free State, guards,
A baker's dozen of them, *bodily*,
My dear good people, put me out of bed
And out of first class into third. At two
A.M., do understand. I barely saved
My sample cases. Awkward; terribly."
No train in India, and let alone
In the Oranje Vrystaat, can afford
A force of thirteen guards, but otherwise
Our guest persuades. He is an Indian
Drawing-Room-African, and is preferred
By Houghton hostesses to African
Drawing Room Africans, as, unlike them,
He does not drink. I much prefer him too.
He sees his repertory's up to date;
And what is done to him is done to *him*.
Except that Africans are barred from first,
His story from the train would make the rounds.
I do not doubt that everything that corps
Of diners-out relates occurs. I doubt
It all occurs to them. A true folk art
Encompasses the whole life of the folk,
Accruing as it goes from hand to hand.

"Accosted me, Madame, and took my pass:
For coming here, for coming to this house."
" . . . across the face, and took away my pass,
And took meat pies from my attaché case."
"Aye. Bloodhounds. I was chased. Across the ice."

Fret not. Like Mr. Ghosh turned out of bed
We each must face another province quite.
One thirty years along. True balladeers
Outwit themselves. The anecdotes of slights
And beatings are laid now on their own flesh,
If, that is, canapés six nights a week
Did not undo them first. And Samir Ghosh,
Pale hands, pink-tipped, like lotus buds that float,
Where are you now? Who lies beneath your spell?

Who lies beneath your spell, where are you now?
Crushing out life, or waving in farewell?

The Incorruptible

(Kansas City)

A lot of Sodom in a little rain,
Sin's most accomplished City of the Plain
Sits on its ridge. A high-school band in tow,
I doze on board a school bus. How atone,
Who am the world's last living chaperon.
Hotel rooms—eight—the boys on one and two,

The girls on high floors undisclosed, and pray
Their elevators fail. Though I must pay
For steak, thereafter they are on their own,
The shy to search the nearest pusher out,
The bold to stammer, at the hooker. Rout
Or triumph, harder rain must send them home,

Free, wet; and poker on the second floor
Be all their sin. It keeps us up till four.
Tomorrow, on a pristine Astroturf,
In uniforms that are a bright echo
Of Österreich-Ungarn, a heartland show,
They will compete for two weeks in the surf,

And, being sleepy, lose. Outside of town
The Zoar local overheats, breaks down.
It is a judgment. In the endless halt
To change the hoses they do not look back.
There is no fire, no brimstone; only wreck,
And in the nearby roadhouse, ice-cream salt.

Accruing judgment in hotel bedrooms,
The city of the low escarpment looms,
And for survivors notoriety
Is to have been there. Look behind or burn,
In their good time they marry. If they turn,
It's into Pillars of Society.

Betsy Ross, Astronaut

Moon vehicles so far devised,
If they resemble anything,
Resemble High Victorian
Sewing machines: a bobbin (no,
Not Yeats's; Singer's), eyes of steel,
Iron "limbs," an oblong treadle placed
However. We who have a sense
Of things suspect deep down our crews
Stitch up en route the flags they plant.

Streamline, Designers, and if air
Resistance is in outer space
No factor, streamline still. The Deco
Objets on the *étagère*
May never move, but let space-time
Fall on them in its utter storm
And they will sleekly be prepared.
The heart, which mainly is a pump,
Has grace not to resemble one.

Some People Have No Small Talk

From isolation to the dart board, a trajectory
Of social distance, barroom Concorde replicas have aim
And fly. Who throw them, having failed to replicate so much
As a synthetic self, enjoy, or settle for, a least
Companionship the game provides. It comes, conclusively,
To this kind fact: the lowest score is not quite nothing. Darts,
Intended or at random, on the mark or off the wall,
Make good the arc and are a concord: link forged beyond sound.

Lazy Afternoon

No doubt to dream his fleas will take to felt,
A yellow dog lies on the one pool table
Which is the amenity. Just how
So mange-imbued a presence lets a bar
Maintain its self-respect is less than clear;
Its hint, perhaps, that alcohol is *not*
The clientele's best friend; or that there waits
Beyond the skids the fate of Jezebel.
"Out! Out, Hyaena," Milton says (Lamar
Q. Milton, who tends bar) and as the dream
Now shatters racks his last eleven balls
As if to deal with fleas by crushing. Nose
Stuck in a pocket, Hy goes back to sleep.
And, noses in their beer, the regulars
Doze also. The beer warms; the beer cans sweat.
The air-conditioning cannot cope either.
Random in the moment's mind that copes
A circus goes: an itch among the wool,
A minute demonstration under glass
To the effect all motion's Brownian—
This eye that sees; the tongue that calls for drink;
The shark who has the break; the luck, the fleas.

Campion in Uniform

Error predates computer error. Quite
Through manual incompetence alone,
Our mess-hall has received a year's supply
Of Queen Anne cherries. Breakfast, lunch, at break
Or in the field, we dine on Royal Anne.
The thought is still enough to make one gag.
God did not mean His cherries to be white.

The gag reaction is most fiercely high
In years when lipstick, fashion says, is pale.
In Basic Training, if one thought of lips,
It was in terms of maraschino red.
Most Stuarts, dropsical or dull and gross,
Missed great careers as warrant officers.
Ripe, cherry ripe, what can a Queen Anne cry?

For the Scrapbook of
Mrs. Charles Black

Columbia, South Carolina, in October,
1952. The iron palmetto, symbol
Of a symbol, arms the lawn, the statehouse steps,
Somewhat as if the Krupps had turned to gardening,
Or Vulcan left behind a giant swizzle stick.
But what to swizzle? In a suicide revenge
On servicemen, downtown is dry. Intense research,
However, presently reveals there is a bar—
It seats four—lost in the Columbia Hotel.
Two drinks are legal. Not, you understand, two drinks
Per person. Two *kinds*. One can have a champagne cocktail,
Sugar cube and all, or have a Shirley Temple.
How, pray, can an adult man, in uniform
Unman himself by ordering a Heidi-Ho
In public. Try the U.S.O., and lukewarm beer?
No, anything but other servicemen. And, for
The moment, I am not in public. I'm alone.
"I'll have a champagne cocktail." May a draftee's curse
Turn into ash and iron the garden clubs and gardens
Of this ladies' luncheon town. Cheers.
                                   Enter now,
Internal exile written on their faces, she
Who past all doubt was the outstanding shot putt star

Of Carolina High; and the Platonic, fixed
Idea of a failed interior designer.
"Wet a cube, Ray. Soldier, I spent every night
From first grade through the fifth in curlers. Hell; fie met
Ole Shirley Temple Agar on the street today
I'd snatch the silly bitch baldheaded. Name's Faye Head.
I do interiors. And here's Du-ane DeWitt.
He drives a truck." It's as it should be, Halloween;
I've found a home.
                          A soldier's blessing, Duane and Faye,
From somewhere in the Caribbean, in the future,
Where the bars are legion and the gardens Eden.
In your desert, as a memory of me,
I pray you get blind drunk. Piss on the iron palmetto.

Mainstreaming

Fort Jackson in the twilight and the coal smoke
Oddly looks like San Francisco, Tank Hill
Being Nob Hill and the mess-hall steps
I sit on any hill that overlooks.
Un-Californian in the extreme,
E Company goes smartly by, then G.
Night training in the field, presumably,
And odds are it's their final. In two weeks
The training cycle ends. I have a scale
Of orders cut that goes from one to ten:
Korea's minus eight; Presidio
Is ten. "And here the Moron Legion comes."
Above me and behind, Mess Sergeant Fay;
And who refers—his slur is literal—
To Able Company, whose Draft Boards have,
In manic zeal to put down Minus Eight,
Inducted borderline retardees. Not
To mince words, Able drools a lot. "Nine weeks
Of Basic," says the Sergeant, "and they still
Can't miter sheets." A bit self-satisfied,
In broken step they march the asphalt streets
As if they crossed a frail suspension bridge.

I have no way of knowing, but I see
A Turk Street of the future: vile fatigues
And leather strapped on the strangest spots.
A look that later age will know as stoned.
It is their cadre whom I notice most;
As if they each one had a shoeshine boy,
A valet, private barber. And a sylph
Who wipes their lips with Kleenex if they drool.

. . . .

"If they discharge them then they have to pay.
Hospital, pensions. So experiment.
It's monkey see and hope that monkey does.
Two-thirds of 'them,' one-third of 'us.' Of course,
If they fuck up then we are punished too.
Ten weeks, and none of us has had a pass.
Don't ask me what my sex life may become."
My confidant is Connor Kennington,
With whom I went to high school. We've an hour
Or so of freedom, in the Service Club.
The Tank Hill Service Club. The Nashville Sound
Is occupation army in our own.
"I'm in the ranks to spite my family.
I write them that I shower with idiots,
And they write back 'But are they White or Black?'"
"That Field First Sergeant's not an idiot."
"Ed Crowley? Yes he is. He had it made
And threw it over. He was acey-deucey
With the Provost Marshal."
                            "AC-DC,
Connor."
            "How would *I* know? I'm a normal.
I'm the one-third. I can make my bed."
"And lie in it?"
                    "I sleep with idiots."

"But are they White or Black?"

                              "Shut up, you mother."

· · · · · · · · ·

Now I sleep with idiots. With two,
Ends up on either side of me, in traction,
In the Base Hospital. I've ptomaine,
But I'm improving. They are burned and blind,
And who could teach them Braille? An accident,
I am informed, last month on the grenade range.
Connor never disappoints. First orders
Cut for Honolulu in a year.
He came by Sunday for a goodbye gloat.
"Pulled out the ring and stuck it up his nose.
Blew up these two, the range instructor, Ed,
Himself, and six observers from Siam.
Aloha. Don't let bubbles in your drip."
I walk him down the hall, and at the turn
We meet a tall young father with a child
Swung on his either crutch. The empty leg
Of his pajama has been neatly pinned,
But crutches are an instant shabbiness.
"OK., you two. Let Daddy learn to walk.
Edwina, reach me up a Kleenex, please.
The tricky part is how to blow my nose."
The children giggle; Connor is all eyes.
"*That* is a family man? I'm not surprised
The Marshal threw him out. M.P. indeed!
Who trusts a man that won't make up his mind?"
"Well, if he takes him back he'll save on spats."

· · · · · · · · ·

Civilian for thirty years or more,
I'm sometimes in the City. In a dusk
Of smoke and traffic, for a second time
Today, my cable car has stalled. In frank
Defeat I sit down on its wooden steps.
Nabobs, how near your hill is, and how far.
Hotels and barracks, idiots and grips,
Nob Hill ahead is grown Tank Hill behind.
A trolley bus, the thinking man's transport,
Rescues us, urging by its postered sides
That one support Brain Damage. Thank you no.
I hear the voice of Connor Kennington,
Echoing, as it were, from Waikiki.
"Ought to be stuck in jars at birth, dumb blobs."
And no doubt, Connor, many of them are.
Tomorrow will be better. Rent a car,
I think, and drive through the Presidio.

Atlantis of the Conchs
I – V

I

Spanish explorers name the island Cayo Hueso—Bone Key—after its littering mounds of Carib Indian remains.

Unkempt, unknown.
An isle of bone.

More islands east;
A dry few west.

Sea-grape and sand,
Mangrove for land

And swamp for water.
Elder slaughter,

White, frail skulls,
Have terns and gulls

Instinctified
Their warping, wide

Command of air
(It picked you bare)

Or learned anew,
As we shall do,

How any fate
Is isolate?

II

Victims of the Maine *explosion are brought from Havana for burial.*

On darkened sleeping-porches
Light of fresh pine torches:

Torchbearers in the streets,
And in their winding sheets,

On canvas stretchers, numbered,
The soon to be remembered.

How the house of plague,
However facts be vague,

Enjoys the chalk, the X,
It by and by rejects.

"Recall," the line will go,
"USS *Alamo.*"

And in the morning, bedding,
Shutters, insect-netting,

Sharp with smoke and pine,
Have honeysuckle vine.

III

*The construction of the Overseas Railway alters the course of the Gulf
Stream and changes the climate of Western Europe.*

Themselves horizon, and its haze
They either seem or seem to raise,

The arches and the trestles, new,
Divide the undividing blue.

Already, hot by wide stone piers,
The violated current veers.

Up there, in ice that never ends,
High glaciers move. And where the sands

Stretch out from Calais, toward the cliffs
That are in dreams the edge itself

Of ice age, ice as real as stone
Creates a right-of-way to own.

Iron Suez of the frozen Channel,
Cheap rails make obsolete the Tunnel.

IV

The WPA turns the Keys into a major tourist attraction of the Depression.

In vehicles that travel only south,
We camp from isle to isle and hand to mouth.

You South downhill from Ozarks and from Smokies,
Cockroach Country, greet us Counter-Okies.

California ceases at the pier;
The sea itself drops off six miles from here.

One town with just two things to do. No more.
Become a sailor or become a whore.

My wife gets seasick; I'm not very cute.
The tourists fish a lot; we'll follow suit.

The coffee's Cuban and the pie Key Lime.
Right now it's "Sailor, can you spare a dime?"

V

Hurricane Maude destroys Key West and the wicked are punished.

Out of the Dry Tortugas gusts and driving rain.
The sea is rising. In the blacked-out shrines of gain

Their broken fan blades circle in the wind they were.
The wigs of drag queens, streaming out in lustrous air,

Quick comets of the eye and storm, fly off. Tatoo
Of arm and tongue of wearer, viper each, are too

The storm-freed snakes of pestilence. The dikes are gone;
The Dutch Boy's dead; the sand is going back to bone.

No action and no scene; no chic; no where it's at.
Beyond the sea's cleft edge there is no Ararat.

Fin de Siècle

The political history of much of the Third World is One Man, One Vote, once.

Rand Daily Mail

Southampton, Bremerhaven, Antwerp . . . No parades
And portholes sealed, hospital ships in guarded docks
Onload: the walking skeletons, quicklime in crocks,
Pets, stretcher cases, eight month pregnant chambermaids.
The nineteenth century is having none of AIDS.

Balfour has died of it; the Household Cavalry
Has been reduced by half. On Flanders waterfronts
It has become "Congo Revenge," and Berlin hints,
In heaping up its pyres, at "Pox Britannica."
Fence wire enough to rim our five main continents

Is bound already for the flats of New South Wales;
In Tanganyika craters will become reserves.
The flag of quarantine, above the world's wide wharves,
Is flying ever yellower. No ship that sails,
Save only these, has certain port. Drug shipments, mails,

Coal, diplomatic bags themselves, wait on the ramps.
Surviving public-school boys go in stowaway;
Archbishops of the Church of England almost pray.
There will be hearts that bleed, and faggots of the lamps,
And very little concentration in the camps.

Will there be greed, and courage in the face of death?
Be for the blind warm steadies, hearers for the dumb?
Be scarred young men whose minds are not on vengeance? Some.
A self served, whole, the century goes out in wrath.
But its decisiveness has saved the twentieth.

The way of presentism is to whore the past
For passions of the moment. That is pestilence
Also. If there are cures, unthreatened lives long hence,
Then what I write is *Masque of the Red Death* at best.
If not, I am the One Good Man in Sodom, once.

Publicans and Sinners

The beach hotel is no house built on sand.
   It is on coral.
The house on rock—at least, that which will stand—
Is Simmons' Lounge. Which would you say, offhand,
   Is more immoral:

Social climbing (my hotel), or slumming?
   At Buddy Simmons'
B-girls at the bar are up and summing;
Pentecostals wait the Second Coming.
   Till Its Summons

All persuasions present have their price,
   As have innkeepers.
Bright green casino felt or grubby dice,
The difference, at last, is imprecise.
I've money I can burn. I need a vice.
   Assault day-trippers?

Franchises

Ezekiel the Prophet dealt in wheels
Within wheels. He did not, one must assume,
Derive a living from it. In this cave
Of chromium, whose walls are disc and wire
And spoke, expertly, Hubcap Annie does.
He is a mild young man whom prophecy
Would not become. You give him year and make,
And option; he will go unerringly
To where that model is. His modest fee
Includes the installation. Like a test
Of knees the rubber hammer swings down twice.
His stocks as yet unsorted chrome the yard.
A fence's fence? Well, let us say Ann takes
His wheels on faith, as did Ezekiel.

Retouching Walker Evans

Every photo—every, every one—
From the Depression having now been found
And anguished over and become the stuff
Of coffee-table books, I see go by
As in an MGM parade of gowns
The bony women in their all but rags.
And on her Shelby, Mississippi, porch,
Reviewing stand of the originals,
My great-aunt Lela, dead for forty years,
Is present as an absent frontispiece.
She is a seamstress some few years retired,
Whose reputation and whose marginal
Prosperity are owed to a device,
Her own, for making over-bosomy,
Notoriously over-bosomy,
Deep Delta women look less so. Her trick:
Bolero-like effects—diagonals
Across the diaphragm and diamonds
Below the arms. A steel dressmaker's eye,
As they head townward on a Saturday,
Takes in the trucks and White sharecroppers' wives,
Who, flat beyond the dreams of any mode,
Contrive to nurse. Each is a gauntlet thrown.

A challenge, as to write backhandedly
Might be for an accomplished forger. And,
Having repeated a bolero theme
As often as Ravel—that other seamstress—
Nature's nemesis now finds herself
Imagining a bertha. Desperate,
But who has seen such gauntness heretofore?
A rival reads her mind. "All right, how *would*
You fill them out?"

                    "A sort of Empire waist
And heavy gathers at the collarbone.
That's all you can do. Short of feeding them."

         . . . .

Between the coffee-table poverty
And now, the first decade to intervene,
The Forties, brings to military wives
Discreet per-diem checks, and to the steel
Eye, trips, nostalgia trips, in the bright form
Of certain Metro musicals. Queued up
For one of these, she is exchanging views
With an exhausted woman who could be,
A few pounds heavier (in Anaheim
The Okies are becoming prosperous
And being hateful to Hispanics), she
Who in the Thirties challenged expertise:
The KKK madonna of the truck.
That expertise a poster now offends.
"Pure, flat-out desperation. In that last one
Even stiff boleros didn't work.
And look at this thing: organdy rosettes
Stuck on her clavicle. Has she no shame?
It's like believing you can call away
Attention from potatoes with a pea.

Of course, in her case nothing *can* be done,
Except for breast-reduction surgery.
If I were head designer do you think
I'd let them put my name on trash like that?"
"Them colors ain't much either," says a voice
In which an expertise may also speak.
"She's Remnant Counter pink and feedsack rose."

Texarkana

Two city halls, and—how it irks—
Two mayors, each with perks.

The jail in Arkansas is small.
In Texas it is tall,

But barely adequate to house
Such cowboys as carouse.

The men back east, that is to say
A hundred feet away,

Have quiet vices, or have none.
Not ever known for fun,

The East is, here as elsewhere, dead,
Dull, dry, and no doubt Red.

Well that State Line Street divides
One town that has two sides

And shows two faces. Has Berlin,
In that split it is in,

Division any more complete?
The checkpoints here, discreet,

Invisible, are, like the Wall,
Not psychological

But surface tension: water, oil.
Not severance: recoil.

Knowledge Is Power,
But Only If You Misuse It

Telepathy does not exist,
And for sufficient reasons: one,
It soon would make society
Impossible, and, two, its cheap
Bypass, in circumventing speech,
Would make sex all too possible,
Which is to iterate again,
It would destroy society.
A fortune-teller's crystal ball
Is blank correctly. Were it not
What need could she have still to work?
No ESP would waste its time
At second-guessing packs of cards,
Unless, of course, the tests were held
In meaningful environments,
That is to say, casinos. Heads
Telepathy will never pierce
Revolver bullets will, and prove
Roulette is Russian, guess is risk.
Whirl, Chamber, whirl! And what is Chance,
That it should make the world go round?
Outside the fragile skull or in,
A future read, our past divined,

More knowledge does not turn the trick.
It is deceit that does: drive wheel
Inside of Fortune's. Cheat who read
The palm so soon of silver shorn,
You know how far to read the mind.

Against Activism

The arch of the fermata holds the note,
If only on the paper. Wrist or breath
Or the depressed piano keys draw out
The sound itself. Inertia audible,
Vibrating string, vibrating air postpone.
That which they so delay, the beat held back,
Is abstract also; yet the mind conditioned
Waits as for the certain thunderclap
Hard on the flash. The lightning, nothing if
Not active principle, creates the wave
Which it anticipates. The lifted felts
In the piano, up-bow, down-bow, tongue
Not touching on the reed, prolong the bars
Each passively, by what they do not do.
Horsehair on catgut takes the active voice?
Of course. The thing the players do not do
Is let the change from down to up-bow sound.
"Free bowing" is the operative phrase.
Assuring linkages by letting be,

Most concertmasters write it in the parts.
Among the brasses faces turn to red;
Arms independent bow one seamless note.
Soon, on the sostenuto, cramp sets in.
The right-hand pedal, all things which sustain,
Do so at least in part by doing nothing.

Arithmetic Equals Numerology

The fact that pi is not an integer
Should tell us what to think of integers
And what to think of pi. Arithmetic
May be, in its strict way, convenient,
But is it *true?* If one and one aren't two,
Are one as a continuum, what then?
A shotgun is as good an instrument
For finding pi as any other. Fire
Some few times at a circle in a square—
A tangent square; count up the bullet holes;
Compare the holes inside to those without.
A rough and ready formula, say you?
Approximation may be all we need.
A pellet, I well know, is not a bullet.
Life, if it is pointed off at all,
Need not reach out to ninety decimals.
It stops at one, if that's a bullet hole.
And oneness, as I said, goes on and on.

Mathematics Is Never Any Help

On red or black, or heads or tails, the odds
Are always fifty-fifty, as if God's
Mandate ran in the even-money bets.
One counts; the silver in the air forgets.
And if it comes up heads a thousand tosses,
Infinity will randomize. The losses,
However, are in finite time, and ours.
Bound to the wheel, we still have certain powers,
Among them that of doubt. The ratio
Roulette embodies or the toss must show
Had first, in ordinary short-term play,
To be perceived, and that means, does it not,
That after too much black, red came a lot.
(I random out tomorrow rhymes I skip today.
Read: extra feet now fall away.)
Eight hits on Liberty or Sitting Bull
Or F.D.R. and one must be a fool
Not to suspect it is a certain plus
To put one's money on E Pluribus.
At nine or ten, however, let it ride.
Is bias not a right of either side?

Other Directed

Two roads diverge, each in a yellow smog.
It is the Freeway. I? I take the one
Most traveled by. It makes no difference,
Nor should it. Eight wide lanes and well-marked turns
Will get you there, without the waste and mud,
Ornate delays of detours. If you know—
Mind, really know—so late itinerant,
Where you are going, is there, now and then,
Some reason not to take the easy way?

Method

The tom-tom in the jungle thomases
Its message; on a mesa in the rear
The signal smokes. Respectively they say
"I'm standing here and beating on this drum."
"I've lit a bonfire; now I blanket it."
Beyond the blunt, beyond the obvious,
What is it possible to say? Is code
Even conceivable in languages
Which are not written? Is the changing beat
Mnemonic? Onomatopoeia? Or—
A parlor-game password—key pre-arranged?
Does fire uninterrupted also speak?
How, tribal poet of the flint and drum
(And your intelligence, I am aware,
Is not inferior to mine) . . . how, bard,
In symbols would you like to have to say
What, at this moment, on this page, this says?

An Attempt to Explain Anorexia Nervosa to Lillian Russell

"It's a disease, Miss Russell, in which girls
And women cease to eat, and starve to death."
"?"
"As many die as whalebone corsets killed."
"!"
"Strawberries Romanoff, Poire Belle Hélène . . .
There is no remedy. It first reveals
Itself in an insatiable desire
To purchase women's magazines. It strikes
High-fashion models, who at least die rich."
"$"
"Psychiatrists also get rich on it,
And architects of vomitoria."
"?$"
"Psychiatrists, Miss Russell, are the heirs
Of patent-medicine practitioners,
With this distinction, that they do not travel.
Here's the menu. Ortolan? Roast duck?
A lobster bisque? Filet of Dover Sole?"
"."

One of the Boys,
or, Nothing Sad
about My Captains

As bellies at the bar, and heads unbowed, unbloodied,
Drink up as men of means the boys I understudied.

No academic has a right to sneer at you, Ducks.
If forced to choose I think I'd pick an honest Ku Klux.

One needs at seventeen a passing public manner.
Mine was no urge to raise a mast, or nail a banner.

The in-group tricks of this crowd were enough. They served me.
They may, from certain traps, uniquely have preserved me.

You cannot know, subcultures, artists, mixed assortments,
How *you* may have to learn the tongue of trust departments.

All you who garner fresh rejection slips, or lack mail
Altogether, do you write from sheer self-blackmail?

All sports intensely bore me, if they are not bloody.
The Country Club, however, is a richest study.

I scorn, from my guest vantage, nervous, job, class tensions.
I work the here, the now; work it in three dimensions.

One cannot say my erstwhile cues, my captain-models
Shine like stars. They certainly were not my idols.

Still, they had their moments. Less is more. And "I,"
That inner self whose effort was to slip it by,

Undoubtedly they see. The Bridge must type and rank you.
The inner me on view? He's doing nicely, thank you.

Links

My young grandfather, for the me of four,
Blew smoke rings. I, these long years more,

Without much gift, can, nonetheless,
Redeem my breath from utter shapelessness.

I have no grandsons, having had no sons.
Still, it is good to know that as he once

Made fire his speech and bridged a clinging void,
However differently employed,

I sometimes smoke a little too,
And might bring off the tricks he used to do.

Invitations

Prosperous,
but in the neighborhoods I knew
   well on the way to shabby,
where I lived, a *déjà vu*
   I put from sight to tip the cabby,
    also costs.

   A Bosporus
partitioning Byzantine teens
   from footstool shores of fifty,
time and damp estrange the scenes
   I move through in my tourist mufti.
    Safe from frosts,

   unused to wine
and used to mildew, Fall at home
   is these at-homes; is egg
nogs served in rooms of course too warm.
   Be it the measure of the dregs
    of dullness, that,

at fifty-one,
as guest, I count as an event.
    Is there so little left
of what we were that I am it?
    Is there no trace, behind the heft
        and money, debt,

        fur coat on credit,
facelift fallen, of the high
    ambition and the well
meant willingness to learn and try—
    conform, yes, yet have still
        our selfhood? "Edit?

    No, I write." It
makes afternoons like this quite central.
    Fruitcake? I think not;
I read it—as a sweet, small entrail:
    Be very careful what you want,
    for you will surely get it.

Open Wounds

One test infallible, one only measure
   Of a loss that never passes:
     Ask the loser
Does he think of it when he must shave.

Of lovers I've cast off I think at leisure;
   Of my enemies (those asses).
     You, my razor
Brings me—you the burn and why I shave.

The morning blade, a masochist's small pleasure,
   Puts my tortures in their classes.
     None the wiser
I, and time no styptic aftershave.

Laying It on the Line

How does a heart of stone
write a love poem?
In free verse, of course,
to show how little rigid
he really is.

I was in love with you
a long time;
I am still.
It calls for no change,
obviously, having been itself
the very "wax lost" that fixed.

You might
want to know, or might
not, that just for you,
just once, I broke my meter.
Such is, as you care
to look at it,
my casual admission of wreck,
or noble Roman
equivalent of opening my veins.
But as you see, the beat keeps coming back.

Random Notes

"**H**edy Lamarr and a Chocolate Bar," p. 3. Gaby, the Parisian heroine of *Algiers* (1938), was the Viennese Lamarr's debut role in American cinema. The release date does not indicate that I am lying about my age. It took movies a while to make it to Mississippi.

"Preservation News," p. 17. Eugène Emmanuel Viollet-le-Duc, 1814–79, "the universal restorer," in Edith Wharton's phrase, restored, as well as Notre Dame de Paris, the walls of Carcassonne, and, as a residence for Napoleon III and Eugénie, Chateau Pierrefonds. In spite of his friendship with the imperial couple, he lost the contract for the Paris Opera to Charles Garnier.

"Ruth Keelikolani," p. 21. The Princess Ruth was a cousin of Bernice Pauahi Bishop, who was the wife of the missionary-banker Charles Reade Bishop and a member of the Hawaiian royal house. Ruth was also, by a step-relationship, a cousin of Queen Liliuokalani, Hawaii's last monarch. In her own right she was High Chiefess of the Island of Hawaii. She was born in 1826 and died in 1883. (The trust which the will of Bernice Bishop funded controls today something like twelve per cent of all the land in the State of Hawaii.)

"On Several Photographs of Nikola Tesla," p. 23. Nikola Tesla, 1856–1943, was born in Croatia, but his parents were Serbian, and Serbia claims him. The degree to which Edison and Marconi were in his debt is still being argued, as is the nature of his relationship with Anne Morgan, daughter of J. P. Morgan the elder.

"Inducted," p. 25. *Çay,* i.e. tea, the Turkish national drink. *Kahve* (coffee) is relatively expensive in Turkey. What we call Turkish coffee is in fact Arabian.

"Power Failure," p. 32. At 3025 carats in the rough, the Cullinan Diamond, discovered in 1905, has not been exceeded, although the nature of its crystal structure suggests that it was part of a larger stone, as yet unfound. Thomas Cullinan was founder and board chairman of the Premier Mine, which is still in operation and still hoping.

"Mainstreaming," p. 48. There are presidios and presidios, but *the* Presidio is in San Francisco. In the 1950s it was regarded as, with the possible exception of the Coast Guard Station in the Virgin Islands, the most desirable military duty in the world.